MW01171604

MYTHICAL MOCKERY

A wizard's field guide to roasts and ridicule

BY

McKenna K. Suman

Featuring genuine sketches, celestial charts,
and alchemy diagrams pulled straight from
medieval manuscripts.

ft.
Painted illustrations
by

Ignis Garcia

ignisGarcia.com
@ignis.g

The art of wizardly roasting is one that precedes even me. it is an ancient technique which i studied and observed in the darkest and dustiest corners of time (i saw it on tumblr). while it is not a concept i have created, it is one i have mastered.

the path to the divine is a treacherous one, filled with many a naysayer. though one's magical prowess is assuredly important, there is another skill set that must be sharpened.

turn thy tongue into a weapon of mass destruction; cut down any who stand in your way. this tome will impart upon you my archaic knowledge of insult.

use it wisely.

Every insult needs a good foundation. To throw taunts around with no rhyme or reason might make one appear a common dunce or town fool. The structure of a proper wizard roast is as follows:

the introduction -

"don't care didn't ask..."

a powerful opener that immediately discredits the libel your opponent has been spewing. To let them know you are unfazed and untouched by their attempt is the first crack in the armor.

the attack -

"plus..."

here is where you will use your artistry of observation to search for weak points. whether it be your opponents appearance, garb, casting, personality, etc... one must lay waste.

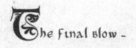

The Final Blow -

"whilst mine..."

as you ravage your enemy's pride, you
must build up your own.
whatever weakness you have locked onto
in the previous step, you must now
explain how it is a personal strength to
you. where they fall, you fly.
affirm your standing as the better
magician and watch it all come crumbling
down.

as your mastery improves, you will gain
the ability to bend this insult structure
slightly to assist your affront.

and with that, i pass onto you my own
personal archive and collection.
may they aid you in your journey.
may they crush the souls of lowly
diviners so that you may walk across
them like stepping stones and rise to
celestial heights.

Corpus
Contumēliarum

don't care didn't ask
plus your prophetic dreams
are seldom accurate whilst
mine always come to pass

don't care didn't ask
plus the quests you give are
meager and unimportant whilst
mine lead to a plethora of
character developments.

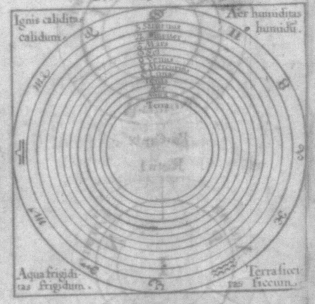

Pro Capite 28

Ignis caliditas
calidum.

Aer humiditas
humidu.

Aqua frigidi-
tas frigidum.

Terra ficci-
tas ficcum.

don't care didn't ask
plus your wand is shoddily
carved whilst mine is
delicately crafted.

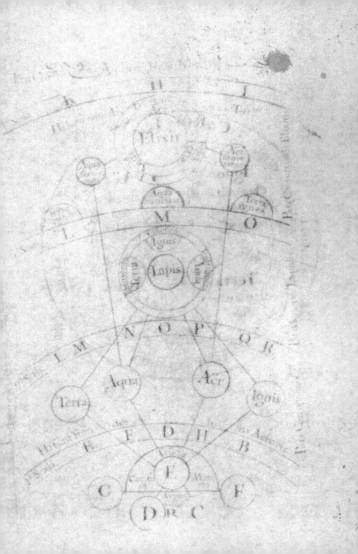

don't care didn't ask
plus your healing potions
give a scant boost whilst
mine revive the fallen.

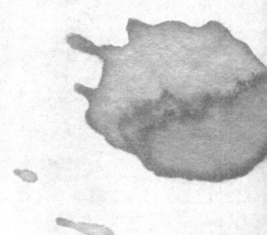

don't care didn't ask—
but your mom did, when she
came seeking my expertise on
time reversal magic.

don't care didn't ask
plus your wizard staff could be
mistaken for a bridge troll's
toothpick whilst mine is
admired as an ornate
legendary weapon

Pro Practica
Cap. 31.

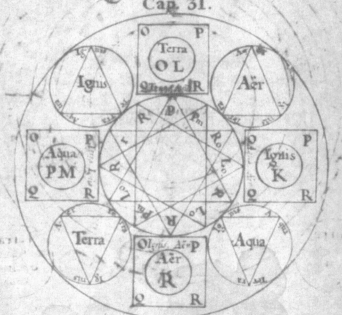

Figura, quomodo ex triangulis & quadrangulis componitur Circularis.

don't care didn't ask
plus the townsfolk dismiss
your ancient wisdom as the
ramblings of an old fool whilst
kings come to me seeking
council.

don't care didn't ask
plus i can traverse the very
wrinkles of spacetime whilst
you cannot even see yourself
out of a conversation nobody
wants you in.

The Hieroglyphical Seal of

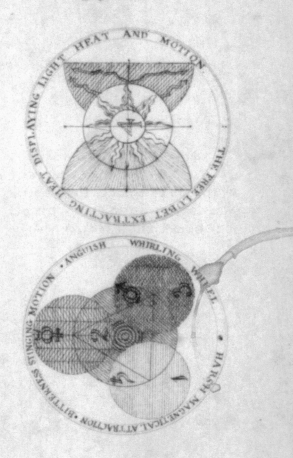

THE TREE OF LIFE EXTRACTING HEAT DISPLAYING LIGHT HEAT AND MOTION

ANGUISH · WHIRLING WHEEL · HARSH MAGNETICAL ATTRACTION · BITTERNESS STINGING MOTION ·

don't care didn't ask
plus your spell book reads like
an adolescent diary whilst
mine will be revered for eons
to come.

don't care didn't ask
plus your wizard hat looks
more like a dunce cap whilst
mine makes me appear wise
and sagely

PENTACOLO MASSIMO

don't care didn't ask
plus your constant craving
for carnal delights clouds your
arcane judgement, whilst i,
unburdened by such
distractions, wield my magic
with purity and focus.

don't care didn't ask
plus the ingredients you use
are reminiscent of low quality
spoils from thine neighbors
garbage, whilst mine are rare,
exotic, and high end herbs. the
likes of which your meager
eyes have never seen.

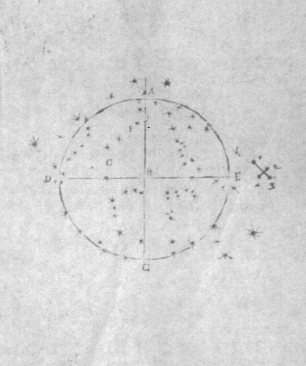

don't care didn't ask
plus your wand crackles with
unstable amateur magic, a
hazard to bystanders, whilst
mine channels the pure
untapped power of the cosmos.

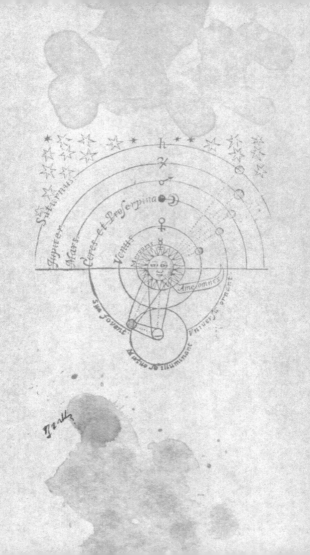

don't care didn't ask
plus your knowledge of the
arcane is meager like a
flicker of candlelight
whilst mine is a blazing
inferno of wisdom.

don't care didn't ask
plus your familiars scutter
about like unruly and mangy
pests, whilst mine are refined
and graceful beings of the
highest pedigree.

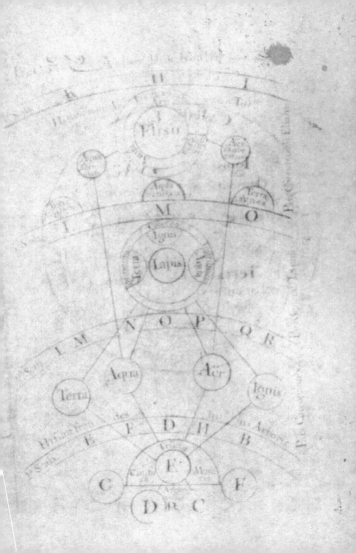

❧

don't care didn't ask
plus we all know you faked
your awakening. You're so
loafing and lackadaisical you
can barely drag yourself from
your bedchamber, let alone
roam the ether.

※※※

don't care didn't ask
plus the salves you brew omit
a foul stench, which even a
man at death's door would turn
away from, whilst mine beckon
with the sweetest aroma.

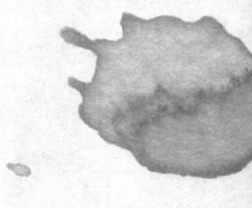

...bilium.

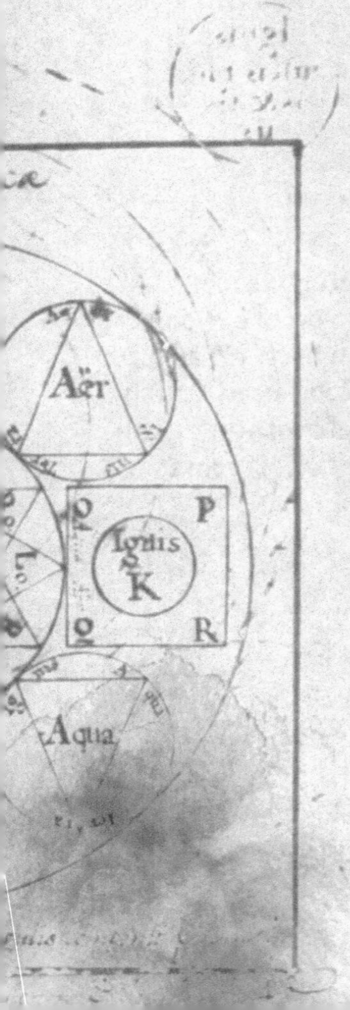

...ca
Aër
Q
P
Ignis
K
Q
R
Aqua

don't care didn't ask
plus, i would offer you a penny
for your thoughts but i fear it
is but a barren wasteland up
there,
which would explain why your
pockets carry nary a sickle.

don't care didn't ask
plus the bards won't even sing
tavern songs about you in jest,
because you're so pitiful it's
not even laughable, whilst
ballads of me are known far and
wide.

don't care didn't ask
plus nobody recruits you for
valiant and daring quests
whilst there are not enough
days in the year to attend all
the journeys i am asked to join.

vp:

Und ein figure b
uesse .

don't care didn't ask
plus your "tragic" backstory
is so tepid even the coffined
corpses can be heard rolling
their eyes from beyond the
grave, whilst mine is so
heart wrenching they have
crafted it into epics and
stage plays.

don't care didn't ask
plus your spectacles are but a
pitiful reminder of your flawed
vision, whilst my eyes are so
powerful they see not only
great distances, but also what
has been and what will be.

don't care didn't ask
plus people consider your
company a stroke of ill fate
whilst they regard my
presence as a divine blessing.

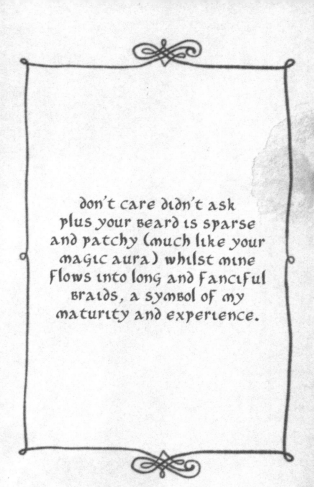

don't care didn't ask
plus your beard is sparse
and patchy (much like your
magic aura) whilst mine
flows into long and fanciful
braids, a symbol of my
maturity and experience.

don't care didn't ask
plus the other wizards laugh at
your wand work, reminiscent of
a troll swinging a toy sword
with reckless abandon, whilst
mine evokes awe and envy.

PENTACOLO MASSIMO

don't care didn't ask
plus your Grimoire calligraphy is
an illegible mess of scribbles and
smudges, a strain to any eyes
which fall upon it, whilst my
script is hailed as a form of art.

don't care didn't ask
plus your magic weaving
technique is that of a spider
spinning a web in a windstorm
whilst mine is the fates
delicately interlacing the very
threads of life.

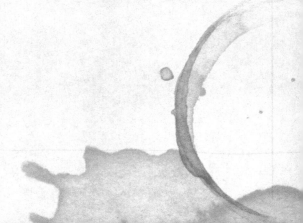

F

don't care didn't ask
plus your literacy of runes is
abysmal whilst i am so savvy
people often refer to me as
the renowned runesman.

don't care didn't ask
plus your vibes are so staunch
you taint the air around you, so
that when townspeople come to
you for readings, you give only ill
omens; whilst i purify and bring
only prosperity and riches.

don't care didn't ask plus
your shoes do not curl up at the
toe with mystical whimsy as
mine do; a mundane and dull
display of magic footwear.

don't care didn't ask
plus your pipe looks as though
it was commissioned by the
town drunk whilst mine is
whittled with precision and
mastery.

don't care didn't ask
plus your crystal ball is so
obscure it may well be a magic
8 ball giving one word answers,
whilst mine shows only the most
elaborate and vivid of visions.

✳

don't care didn't ask
plus your bag of holding could
hold not even a teaspoon of
magic essence (not that you
have that much as it is)
whilst mine is so vast it might
well be the portal to another
world.

...ADORVM + RAON + CLAMA + DALLORA + AORBCRC...

don't care didn't ask
plus your magic mirror is but a
victim imprisoned to your
grotesque presence, whilst
mine is a loyal cohort reporting
to me all the secrets of the
realm.

don't care didn't ask
plus your sorcery is so asinine,
the old king actually thinks you
are the court fool performing a
bit.

The Hieroglyphical of

HEAT AND M

GREAT DISPL

don't care didn't ask
plus nobody invites you to the
round table whilst the very
concept was created around
me, so everyone could have a
clear view of my presence.

※※※

don't care didn't ask
plus your tower is so
decrepit and eerie the
travelers whisper that it
must be the prison of some
poor maiden, whilst mine
is a monument so opulent
and stately it has become
a historic landmark.

don't care didn't ask
plus nobody reaches for your
enchanted sword, rusted rubbish
that seems a terrible safety
hazard; whilst mine is a
captivating beacon of untold
power that beckons the purest
of heroes.

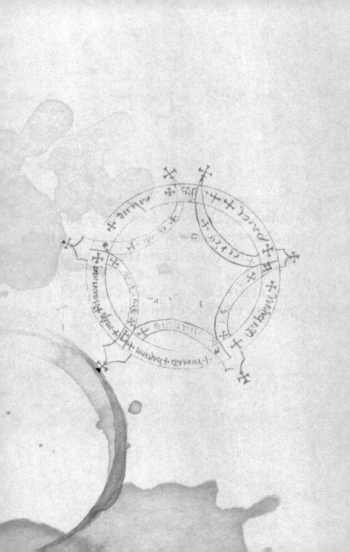

don't care didn't ask
plus your cabinet of
curiosities is so deficient,
the only curiosity it sparks is
the question of why you even
bother, whilst mine is a trove
of so many mind-boggling
creations it leaves scholars
wonder-struck

ἄμπελος μέλαινα
ἐντ...

κουσορρ... αφ φ...   λοτιαρεστ...τριι...

don't care didn't ask plus you
have not a single kingdom in
your debt, as you have
accomplished nothing of
note, whilst i have statues
erected in my image all
across the map.

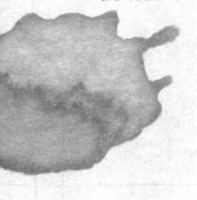

don't care didn't ask
plus your infantine inability to
keep your mouth shut
consistently puts your fellow
Guild members in precarious
situations, whilst i adopt a
mysterious and introspective
air of silence that has people
eagerly awaiting my every
word.

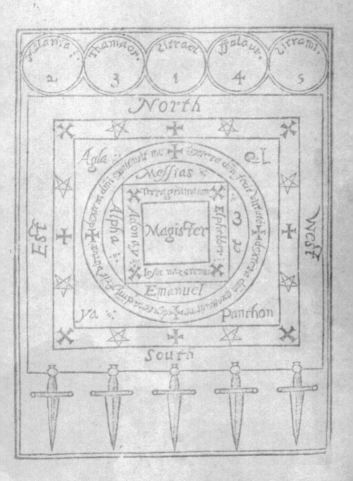

don't care didn't ask
plus your magic portals are so
unreliable they are used as a
form of banishment, whilst mine
are so stable and sincere they
have been dubbed the very gates
of heaven, for which to pass
through is considered
sanctification.

don't care didn't ask
plus your magic staff is
inefficiently and comically
large... almost as if you were
overcompensating for
something, mayhap.

magistrosse mit ans ist den aws schniest... be-
tütte es an daselbe den symne an dem buch
das da heysset das deckstalck an dem teyl
dar man stenet den zwaren oder geuochet an
dem capitel das sich anheket Imperaturis
an dem munde vond an dem buch das da heyset
das decretal an der munde sucht wol an dem
dritten sugel an dem Caplud das sich ver-
libet. Dnia ein Helheut wie wol dinge
symo iurist heschnifft in ditz her erols
schoelst symo woedell sint dis ein empsi
cugit der das liesst dok sich sich das ist hist
vorrgehsten. Dock durch das vollendes
man deste minner anege gesinockten das bit
buch einander gedieckt sol Als man von
den dutschen buchsen deck redes Darumb so
wil ich die selbe eg zezingnung aine cze-
wonlicher hreysten geschrifft. Das su ie-
derhen wird mit Noten nach der linie vnder
stryeheren. Darumb das es dem einfalligen
mit den rwinge so die es zit binder lesen
vnd zit me oschennen doch die gnennige
eunfacher   So wil ich also die
selbe eg zezingnung mit roten stryeten vnd
faren Das es an yeglichen teyles zit lesen
kan deste sichter vberlinden mag werden

don't care didn't ask
plus your cauldron is so vile and
foul it could be mistaken as the
prison chamber pot, whilst mine
is an heirloom of glistening gold.

don't care didn't ask
plus the only way your amulet
could avert evil influence is by
being so ugly it acts as a
natural repellent, whilst mine
is both a dazzling relic and an
extraordinary power of
protection upon its possessor.

don't care didn't ask
plus the academy of magics has
a portrait of you plastered upon
the wall for all to see.........

as a reminder of what failure
and mediocrity looks like, whilst
the entire institution is named
after me as a symbol of my
talent and triumph.

don't care didn't ask plus your
scrolls are so inferior they
are often used as fire
kindling, whilst mine are so
sacred that to lose them would
be akin to the burning of
alexandria.

vp̃
Vnd ain figura b̃
megse

don't care didn't ask
plus your wizard's chalice is so
puny it looks like a Gnomes shot
Glass, whilst mine cuppeth
never runs empty.

Punctus

Terminus a quo
in generatione

In coniunctione

Terminus a quo

Punctus ad quem

Punctus Terminus a quo

Nunc a quo Nunc ad quem

Atque illud recedit ad Nunc a quo

don't care didn't ask
plus... i would say that you
suck at garnering
interspecies unity but
actually, even elves and
dwarves come together in
harmony just to mock you.

...espressia dall' intentione...
...na del conficonato, con te...
...eazione in latina...

ASSIMO

don't care didn't ask
plus your magical maps are
just regular maps— that's how
badly you suck at enchantment.

ΑCΠΑΡΑΓΟC ΠΕΤΡΑΙΟC

don't care didn't ask
plus your aura does not shine
with the effervescent glow of a
thousand stars, as mine does.

Magnum in serpentibus
formis

Mendes

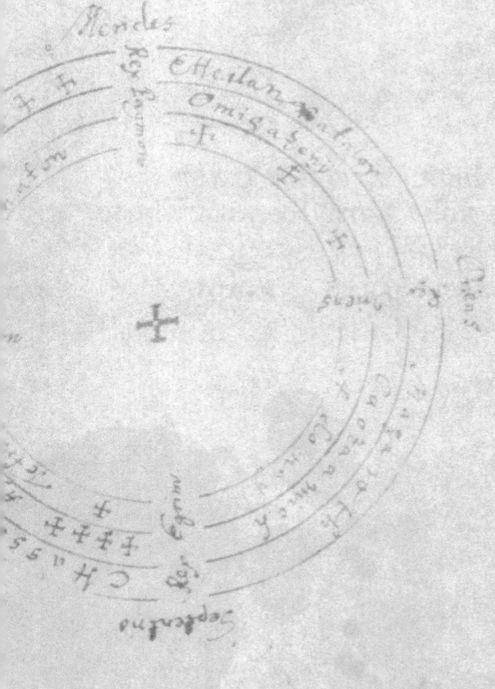

don't care didn't ask
plus you reek with the stench of
mortal rot, whilst i transcend
the confines of fatality.

don't care didn't ask
plus the charade you call
magic is not even convincing
enough to perform at a
child's birthday party;
whilst i am called upon to
demonstrate my power at
grandiose balls and
festivals.

don't care didn't ask
plus your robes are more
bedraggled and wrinkled than a
discarded spell scroll, whilst
mine are silken and sleek like
an elixir from the fountain of
youth.

don't care didn't ask
plus your baby face incites
many a scruple and qualm
about your qualifications as
a grand mage, whilst my
white locks and wrinkles
serve as reminders of my
age-old exploits.

Herba palma Christi
Alchim. 1.

Herba Regulitia. 2.

〰〰

don't care didn't ask
plus, you've read the sacred
texts and forbidden tomes?
You can't even read the room.

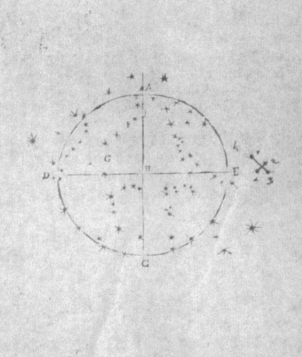

don't care didn't ask
plus no artist will accept
commissions to copy your image
to canvas, as it would be a
hazard on the eyes of the poor
painter, whilst works of me are
considered a craftsman's
magnum opus

don't care didn't ask
plus the man made horrors you
conceive are well within my
comprehension, whilst mine
are so spine-chilling they
could not be imagined by the
human mind.

don't care didn't ask
plus your magically imbued
chainmail is as fragile as your
ego, crumbling to dust at a
single prod, whilst mine can
withstand the sharpest of
blades.

The Hieroglyphical of HEAT DISPLAY'D

HEAT AND

Ignis

don't care didn't ask
plus your roasts are so flaccid
you might best stick to casting
fireball in an attempt to lightly
singe someone.

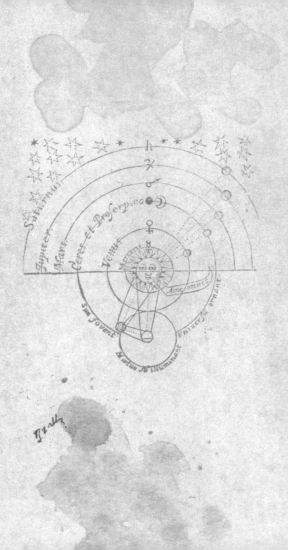

don't care didn't ask
plus the hood of your cloak doth
not conceal you in an air of
intrigue and mystery, as mine
does.

geschryfft ont me yst den ... schmep ... be
den syrne an den

hebt ... ein Schent wie
syne furste heschryfft

magt werden

don't care didn't ask
plus the only curse you're
proficient in casting is your own
existence in this world.

don't care didn't ask
plus no young wizard will sign up
to be your apprentice, since the
only lesson you can teach is
tomfoolery and failure.

Demonstratio puncti, & lineæ ab eo more mathematico profluentis.

Punctus

Terminus à quo

In generatione

In corruptione

Terminus ad quem

Terminus à quo

Punctus

Punctus ad quem

Nunc à quo   Nunc ad quem

Atque illud recurrit ad Nunc à quo

don't care didn't ask
plus you cower away from dark
magic like a child without a
night light, whilst I am such
an illuminated being, I can
wield said magic with no
corruption.

ΑΚΑΠΕΣΑΟΣΙΑ

ΟΡΥΜΝΑΛΑΣΑΡΡΔΙΟΣ

ΑΣΠΑΡΑΓΟΣ ΠΕΤΡΑΙΟΣ

don't care didn't ask
plus your spell-chanting voice
cracks like a prepubescent
boy, whilst mine is rich and
commanding.

don't care didn't ask
plus the people begrudge your
presence so much they take to
assigning you fake tasks just
to keep you away.
Call that a fools errand.

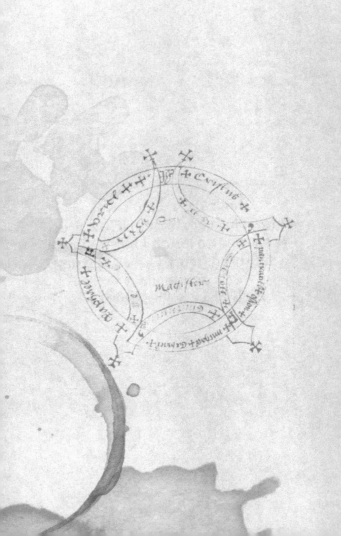

don't care didn't ask
plus your summoning skills
are so null and void you could
not summon me even a single
fuck to give.

¶Le ɟ.liure,

don't care didn't ask
plus you should focus your
time and energy on obtaining
a mastery in transmutation,
perhaps then you could
transfigure yourself into a
better wizard.

With my knowledge now bestowed unto you, i bid you well on your journey.
May these blank pages be the canvas of your own caustic creation.
Remember that wit is the sharpest of all weapons, and an eye for an eye is actually a practical solution that gives you a replacement for the eye which you had previously lost.

x

Lex talionis

Ad Astra

x

Mckenna k.

Made in the USA
Columbia, SC
10 February 2025